HOW PEOPLE FIRST LIVED

HOW PEOPLE FIRST LIVED

by William Jaspersohn

illustrated by Anthony Accardo

A GROLIER COMPANY

Franklin Watts   New York/London/Toronto/Sydney   1985

Library of Congress Cataloging in Publication Data

Jaspersohn, William.
How people first lived.

Summary: Surveys the development of early people
from cave dwellers to users of fire, tools, and lan-
guage, as well as the development of agriculture and
early cities.

1. Man, Prehistoric—Juvenile literature. 2. Civilization, ancient—Juvenile literature. [1. Man, Prehistoric. 2. Civilization, Ancient] 1. Accardo, Anthony, ill. II. Title
GN744.J36   1985   573.3   85-10554
ISBN 0-531-10031-6

For SAMUEL JUDD,
with love

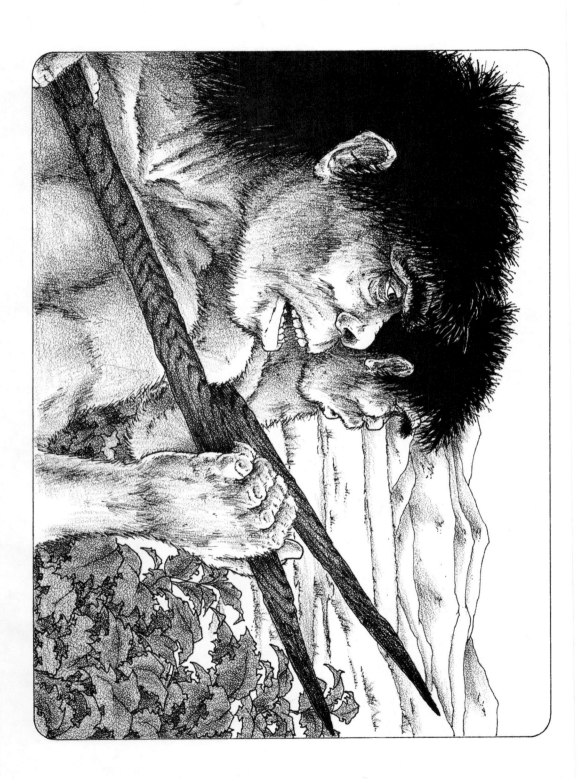

Have you ever wondered
how long there have been people
on Earth?
Do you know what life was like
for the first people?

There have been people on Earth
for a hundred thousand years.
The first people on Earth
were simple ones.

They had no houses,
so they lived in caves.
They had no stores or cars or clothing.
If they weren't careful, they
could be killed by different animals.

So they were careful.
They watched for dangerous animals.
They made weapons from sticks and stones.
They were afraid much of the time.
They stayed together.

They learned that if they were careful,
and if they stayed together,
they could kill animals.
They could eat the raw meat.
The fur could keep them warm.
They were hunters.
They were food gatherers.
They were cold.
Sometimes they still went hungry.
There were many things they didn't know.
One was fire.
The first time people saw fire,
they were afraid of it.
What was it? *Ouch!*
It burned them when they touched it.
It ate wood, leaves, grass.
This was no animal.
Watch out! It could eat *you!*

Later, they learned to control fire.

They kept warm by it.

It helped frighten away strong beasts.

They dropped meat in it by mistake.

They ate the hot meat.

It tasted good!

They learned that cooked meat was better than raw.

They learned a lot of things.

They learned how to trap animals and then spear them.

They learned how to shelter themselves with sticks and grass.

They were finding out that if they *thought* about a problem, they could solve it.

They were becoming problem-solving people.

One of their problems
was how to move big loads.
They could push them.
They could pull them.
But pushing or pulling a load
over long distances
was hard.

Someone had an idea.
Who was he?
We don't know.
He put logs under the load
that he wanted to move.
The logs rolled.
The load moved easily
when it was pushed.

Those logs were really
the world's first wheel.
Later, people took the idea farther.
They cut ends off logs
and mounted them on poles.

They made carts
that could carry things.
Life was a little less hard
because of the wheel.
The wheel was a great achievement.

Other achievements followed.
People began to capture animals
and raise them for meat and milk.
This process of capturing and raising

is called *domestication*.

Cows, goats, horses, pigs, sheep, hens, and ducks—these were the animals that early people domesticated.

In some lands there were elephants,
and people domesticated them.
Some people domesticated dogs—
sometimes for meat, but mostly for
protection and companionship.
People were changing.
Some were still hunters who
roamed the lands in search of food.
But others were becoming farmers.
They lived in crude houses.
They domesticated animals.
They planted seeds and watched
them grow.
And when there were plants,
they harvested them.

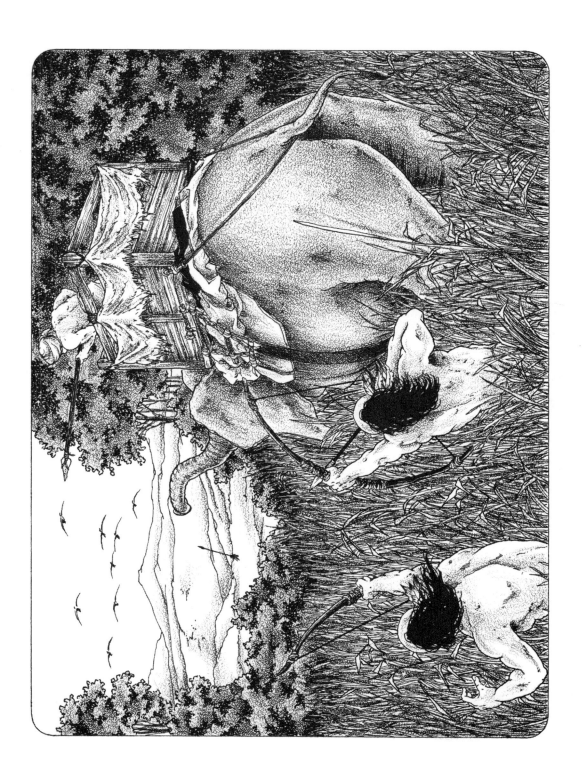

What a difference it made

not to have to travel so far for food.
Farmers could concentrate on other things—
like making tools and building houses
and raising families.
Farm families could live near each other
and protect each other from dangers.
They could share ideas.
They could learn from each other.
One thing early people learned
was how to work with metal.
Their old friend fire helped them
to find metal and later to heat it
and shape it into tools.
Metal tools and weapons
were better than stone tools.
They lasted longer.
They didn't break so easily.
They were stronger and sharper.

Other things, like clay jugs
for carrying water, nets for fishing,
and ovens for baking and cooking,
came later. But tasks were becoming
a little less hard. People had more time
to dream and wonder.

They wondered about so many things—
what that hot dot in the sky was,
why it disappeared at night,
what those bright things were
that twinkled in the darkness.

They didn't know.
They didn't know why it was hot
some of the time and cold other times.
They didn't know
why water fell from the sky.
These things amazed them!

Some things, in fact, were so amazing
that they frightened people.
People saw that the frightening things
had powers that could hurt them.
They thought that the frightening things
were powerful spirits.

They made up stories about the powerful spirits.
They were careful around them.
They gave the spirits food
and clothes to keep them happy.
Sometimes the gifts worked.
Other times the spirits got angry anyway.

There was so much to talk about—

how an animal had been slain,

how the crops grew best,

what happened to people when they died.

Some people were better at talking about

these things than others.

They had a way with words.

They enchanted their friends and families

with stories of this and that.

These people who could talk so well

were the world's first *storytellers*.

From the earliest times, too,

people had drawn pictures to show what had

happened to them.

The pictures were like stories.

The people who drew and painted them

were the world's first *artists*.

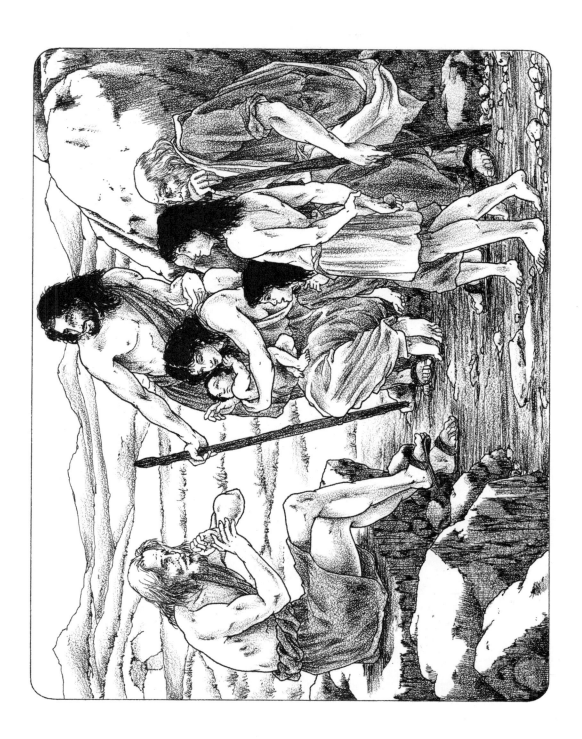

The world's first sailors
were people who floated on logs.
At first they didn't go very far—
they were afraid, and they didn't know
how to swim.
But then they hollowed the logs.
They invented boats.

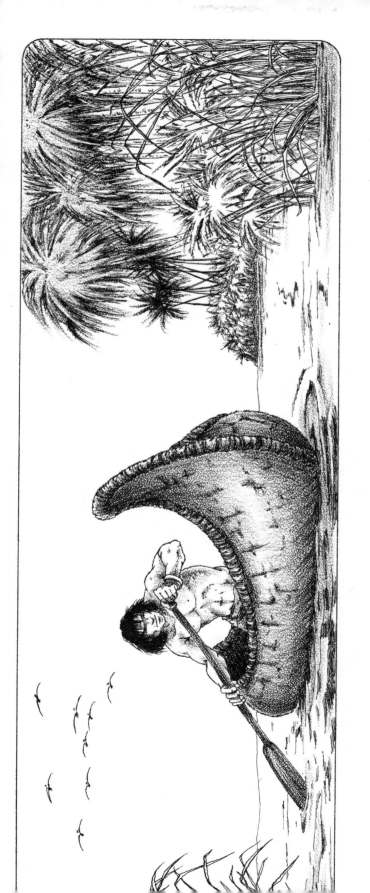

They poled and paddled these boats.
They made bigger ones.
They invented sails. The boats moved fast.
With boats they could travel farther.
They could go to new lands.
They could meet new people.
Sometimes these meetings weren't friendly.

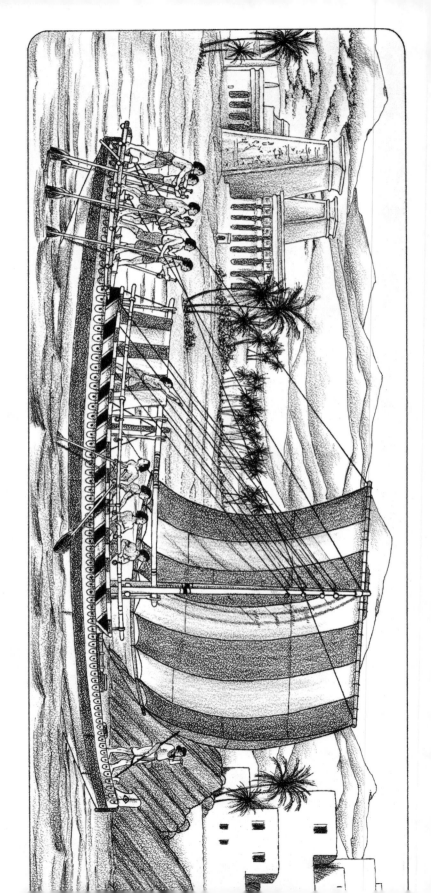

People began to settle more
near lakes, rivers, and streams.
That way, there would always be water
for crops and drinking.
Travel was easier; people used boats.

Groupings of people and houses called *settlements* formed near many rivers.

Some settlements grew as more people came.

The settlements grew into towns.

And some settlements grew into cities.

Life in these towns and cities was busy.
People were doing many different things.
The ones who worked best with metals
became blacksmiths. The ones who worked
best with clay made pots. Those who
were good with tools built different things—
boats, wagons, and houses.
People's work became more and more
specialized.

One problem many people had
was keeping track of how many things
they built or raised or traded.
How many sacks of grain
did the last harvest bring?
How many bricks did the builders need
for a house?
There had to be a way to keep track.
And there was!

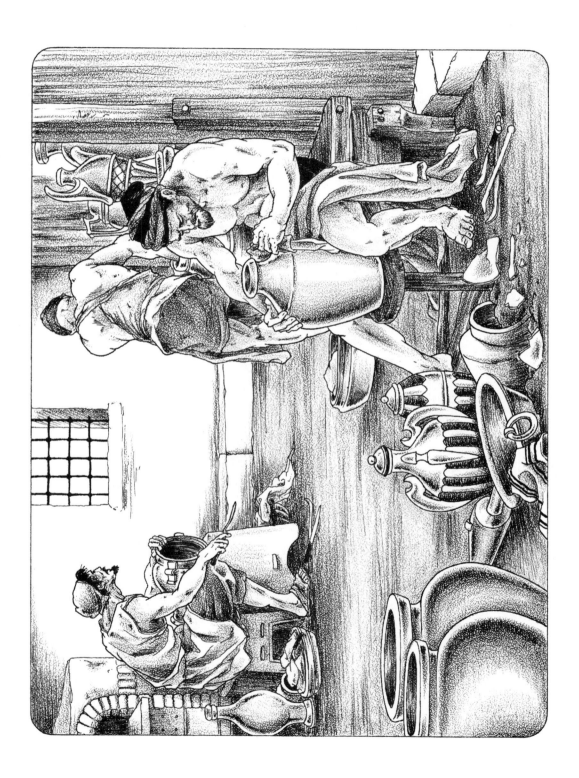

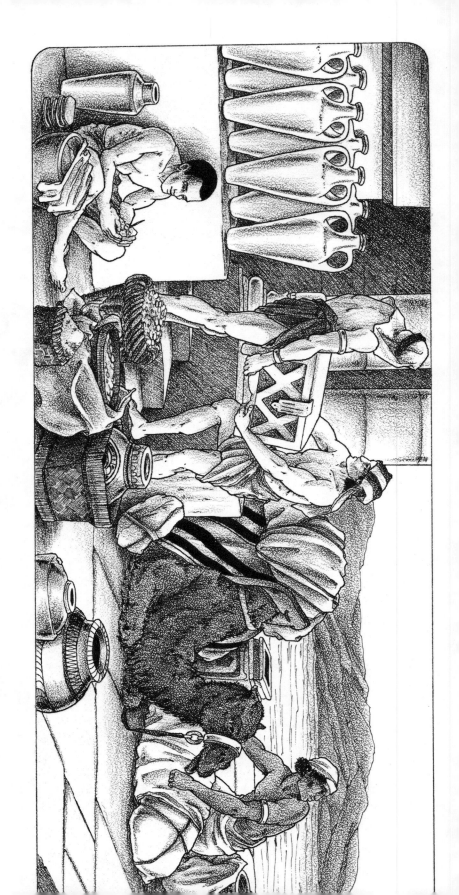

People could scratch little marks in the dirt, one scratch for each thing that they counted. This was the world's first *number system*. Later, somebody made the marks in wet clay.

These clay slabs, called *tablets*,
could be dried and kept a long time.
They were like pages.
Each page held different *information*.

Soon life became so specialized
that certain people had only one job—
to write on those clay slabs.

These people were called *scribes,*
which is another word for *writer.*

Scribes needed different marks
to keep track of different things.

At first, they drew simple pictures.

This picture ♉ meant "one sack of grain."

This picture ♉ meant "one jug of wine."

This picture ⛵ meant "ship."

And this picture ∽⊙ meant "fish."

40

But the pictures took too long to draw.
Simpler pictures were needed.
So scribes drew simpler pictures.
Before long, the pictures looked completely
changed. They didn't look like fish or ships
or wine jugs.
They looked like blips.
The looked like squiggles.
The scribes knew what each squiggle meant.
They had invented something.
That something was *writing!*
Writing made it easier
to keep track of things.
Scribes worked more and more
on their writing.
They thought, "Wouldn't it be nice
to write the words we say?"

But how could they do it?
By inventing an *alphabet*.
An alphabet was a system of sounds.
Each sound was different.
By stringing the sounds together,
the scribes could write words.
Early alphabets were different,
depending on where in the world
they were invented.
Now people could communicate with each other
in different ways. They invented
systems of numbers, too,
so they could count
and measure things better.
People knew so much more now.
And the more people knew,
the more they *wanted* to know.
They had a thirst for knowledge.

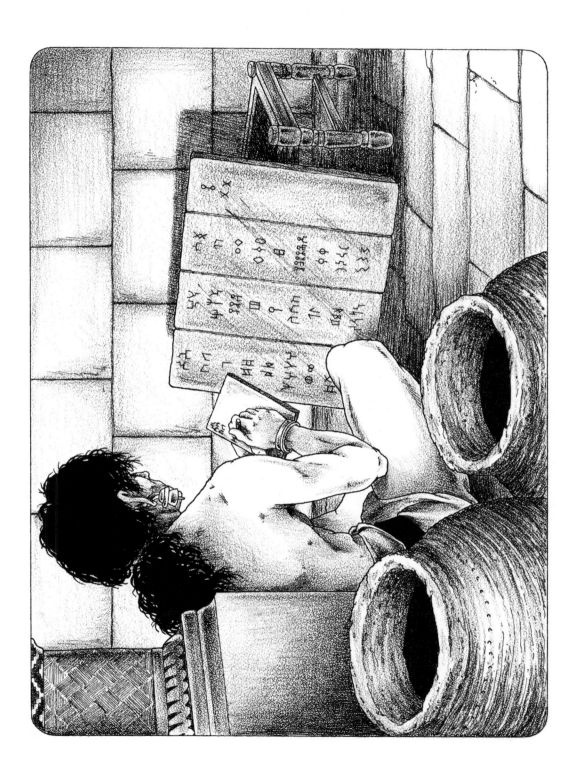

But—oh!—
they thirsted for power, too.
They wanted lands that belonged to others.
Sometimes they hated their neighbors.

Some neighbors had different ideas from theirs.

Some neighbors believed different things.

Some people fought wars with other people over these differences.

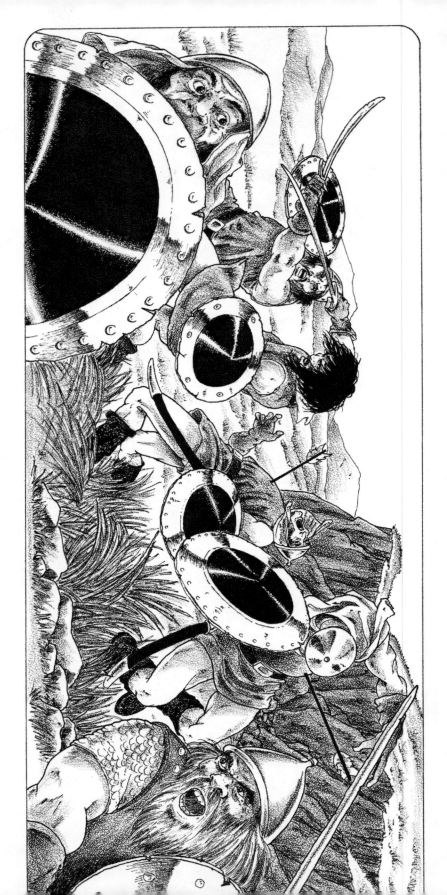

Some of the wars
destroyed entire countries.
People were killed
or forced to become slaves.

Powerful nations rose and fell
as wars were fought for different reasons.
Today, wars are still being fought
in the world.

We have learned much
since the days of the early people.
We still invent,
discover and explore.
Our problems are greater,
and our wars are a bigger danger.
But we know we can live together—
without war—
if we try.